THE COMPLETE WEBSITE PLANNING GUIDE

A STEP-BY-STEP GUIDE FOR WEBSITE OWNERS AND AGENCIES ON HOW TO CREATE A PRACTICAL AND SUCCESSFUL SCOPE OF WORKS FOR YOUR NEXT WEB DESIGN PROJECT

DARRYL KING

ireckon
publishing

Published by Ireckon Pty Ltd

Requests to publish work from this book should be sent to
publishing@ireckon.com

National Library of Australia Cataloguing-in-Publication entry : (paperback)
Creator: King, Darryl, author.
Title: The complete website planning guide : a step-by-step guide for website
owners and agencies on how to create a practical and successful scope of
works for your next web design project / Darryl King.

ISBN: 9780648053705 (paperback)

Subjects: Website development--Handbooks, manuals, etc.
Websites--Authoring programs.
Websites--Design.
Web publishing.

CONTENTS

INTRODUCTION

Have you wondered how to get the absolute best out of your business (or organization) website?

Do you want to be able to have more control about the end result and how well it will work but not be the website builder?

Do you need to rebuild or build your first website and have no idea where to start?

What you need is a simple website planning method that walks you through planning, designing and building your next website!

WHAT CAN YOU LEARN HERE?

This **step-by-step process** will walk you through everything you need to know to create the plan you need to clarify what you **want** from your website, what you

need from your website, and enable you to choose better who to work with and how to know if you got what you asked for.

This is our guide from over 17 years of scoping and building websites and web applications; that lays out clearly for you how to create your own scope and take control of your website success.

This guide won't teach you how to build websites as a designer, but it will help you get the right designer **to build the site you want** and need to make your business results grow the way you want them to. It won't teach you every skill in depth on the particular modalities like Usability and Information Architecture, but it will give you the starting points for all of these that you can expand on.

The result will help improve what you do at whatever level you are, and can be expanded on and utilized as a document template even for experienced teams wanting a more thorough plan for their clients.

WHO IS THIS GUIDE FOR?

This guide was designed for **Business Owners, Marketing Teams**, and Managers that have the responsibility for their business website

Anyone in an organization that has the role of running their current website, **planning their next website upgrade** or **building their first website** will benefit from this process.

If you need to work with developers and designers to build your site then this will help both you and them in creating a better website.

This guide was also made so that other developers and designers can use it to help them work better with their clients. Not every agency or developer has the capacity or desire to build out scopes of work for the sites they build, many would love a clear set of guidelines and marketing information to help them do what they do better.

You only have to read the 'Clients From Hell' website to see there is a lot of frustration on the supplier side. This guide will **help remove that frustration**.

We believe that a consistent approach for all will help both provider and client get better results, with much more information up front and the removal of significant assumptions and guess work.

This can be used internally within an organization as well as with external providers. The guide should help everyone remove the missing piece in planning for successful websites.

WHY IS THIS GUIDE NEEDED?

Ask most business owners or marketing executives about their experiences in building corporate websites and you will hear many stories about the difficulties, frustrations, and problems they have.

Many people refer to websites as **an "IT" thing** (yes — still) despite it being one of the most **critical marketing and communication tools** they have.

On the developers side there is still massive frustration concerning how to best get specifications, requirements and all the essential information up front so they can accurately estimate and quote projects, but also to provide transparent and realistic information on the key client questions of how much, how long and what will we need to do.

Everyone will get better results!

From Business Owners to Freelance Developers, Agency Teams, Marketing Managers or Assistants, General Managers of medium businesses, small teams to big company project groups, by using a structured clear human-focused scope of works.

After more than 20 years spent working with businesses and organizations of all size and their websites and applications, enough was enough!

Over the lifetime of our business, our team members cried out for better scopes and clearer information and we were forever looking for and improving on what we did. It never seemed quite enough. There were always too many shortcuts or missing pieces of critical information that showed up late in the process of development that should have been discovered earlier.

Everyone gets so excited about a new project that all the energy goes into a push to get started and finished without taking the necessary steps.

Many small and medium businesses don't have the breadth of skills to help them and rely on the development team (like ours) too much to help guide them. Not every company has access to Online Marketing stars across areas like Information Architecture, Usability, and Customer Journey Mapping, to Content Management and Development.

So a blueprint was needed to help step people through a process.

If you care about your website, then this guide will help you plan, build and get better results from it.

This book is set out in three key areas:

1. AN INTRODUCTION

Start at the beginning and grasp why a process like this matters.

Understanding the core concept behind a proper brief and some of the common mistakes will help you think through each step and why it is important to you.

Chapter 1: What is a website brief/scope?

Chapter 2: Common Mistakes.

2. THE FOUNDATIONS

Get these foundations done right and your site will have a very solid structure to build on. You get to choose whether you build your structure on sand or rock.

Setting goals for your business and the website helps you understand what you need from your site. Determine who your best clients are and how to help provide them solutions. Identify items you simply can't do without which will help to provide you the base on which to build the site.

Following up with relevant research at vital stages in the process will complete the core information you need to go and create a meaningful website.

Chapter 3: What's the result you want?

Chapter 4: Who's your audience?

Chapter 5: Your business must-haves

Chapter 6: Research

3. THE BLUEPRINT

This is equivalent to architectural drawings in construction, where you flesh out the structural detail that matters most. What will go where and why, and what will it say.

The bulk of the work that goes into making a useful brief that allows you to dictate the result you want is done through this stage.

Step-by-step instructions on drawing sitemaps, writing out the page scopes, how to wireframe (or get wireframing done right), the role content plays and how to address it.

Finally bringing all of this together into a useful brief document or scope of works for your website project that can be shared and used to choose your development team.

You become the architect of your ideal new website.

Chapter 7: Drafting a Map

Chapter 8: Scope it out

Chapter 9: Wireframing

Chapter 10: Content is King

Chapter 11: The Final Document

2

WHAT IS A WEBSITE BRIEF OR SCOPE?

A website scope of works is a document that can fully explain your business needs and requirements in a practical way, used by designers and developers in quoting and building a website.

A website scope is simply a blueprint for success. It's a thought-out set of drawings and specifications that allows you to get the exact result you want, or better.

The foundations of any good web project start with proper planning. A website brief should be extensive enough to provide answers to almost every question a developer or business manager might ask about your project.

Do You Have A Template?

When I ask new prospects about a brief for their new site the most common question I hear is, "Do you have a template I can use?"

Many companies have some form of a list of questions or even more advanced documents, but few if any are available that help the client provide the developer a useful brief up front.

We hope that by providing a sensible template, and the process to complete it, more clients will be able to think through and better design what they want and need for their business, helping produce a better result from the development teams they engage.

Learning to scope and brief what you need for your business will greatly improve your business website, and will naturally start to include many principles that lead to more extended areas of online marketing.

Where Does It Fit In?

When you start looking at the process of building a website and what you might need to do to make it a high performer for your company, you will find there is a myriad of 'specialties' or areas to consider, and everyone is selling the perfect method to help you!

Advice Is Everywhere

Articles, tools, ebooks, courses, training programs and agencies all exist to show you how to market your business better. They will include all sorts of areas, for example Conversion Optimization (CRO), Search Engine Optimization (SEO), Pay per click Advertising (PPC), Lead Pages, Usability/User Experience (UX), Customer Experience (CX), the list goes on.

The Problem

All of these are vital in the ongoing marketing of your business, especially as the site gets more mature and you understand how to manage it better.

The biggest problem is that in many ways this is treating the symptom, not the cause.

These focus areas are often applied after the fact, when all of the work is completed and the site already built, and then you start to hear responses like this, 'Our CMS won't do that' when you want to make a change for the better.

You also can't afford to apply a tactic to your site simply because of a new ebook or blog you read without understanding the impact to YOUR business. You need to have a roadmap/guide about your site that allows you to make smart decisions on what can and can't be implemented, or more importantly what should or shouldn't be applied.

This Complete Website Planning Guide aims to understand your immediate needs now at the beginning of the process, as well as your long-term needs during the lifetime of your site.

You become the architect of your new site and get to design how it will work!

> *"Design is a plan for arranging elements in such a*
> *way as best to accomplish a particular purpose."*
> *-Charles Eames*

Become An Architect.

Let's relate a website scope to something many of us can understand – building a home.

The role of the architect in building a home is huge. Behind the scenes, they have helped to determine need, practicality, wish list items, costs, and numerous other items, then they lay them all out into a schematic and plans that can be used by others to create the result for the client. They will engage other specialties to help as well.

When someone asks me to give them a ballpark figure for their website I often respond with this question:
Do you want a one-bedroom simple studio villa or a two-story five bedroom McMansion?

Both can be considered homes, but the cost and time to build them both will vary massively.

The style of each will be significantly different and what the end expectations are will also be vastly different. That question just touches the surface as there are many other issues that you need to consider.

The materials, will it be block, wood or steel? What type of roof, internal walls, finishes, paint colors? Every one of these decisions impacts how successful the project is on completion. Understanding the project details before you start whether it be building a home or a website is a proven method to being successful.

Learn From Grand Designs.

If you have ever watched a show like *Grand Designs* then you know how easy things can, and do, go wrong, causing cost blowouts, requirement changes late in the piece, and dissatisfaction from the owner.

When you see a *Grand Designs* project with major issues, you can usually find at the core one or more of the items listed.

In many cases starting a construction project without an adequate plan leads to poor results and the majority would be greatly improved if better planning was involved.

While it isn't always the case and many web projects run

smoothly without any plan, the majority would and should be better if better planning was involved.

A successful web project is very similar with many of the same components to it and potentially many of the same problems that can occur.

Builder Problems on *Grand Designs*:

- No experience
- Not taking onboard professional advice
- Trying to do complex work themselves
- Not using an architect
- Not setting fixed parameters
- Lack of compromise on items that lead to cost blowouts
- Poor choice of builder
- Not getting appropriate approvals or simply not following them
- Not enough research/investigation

A scope is simply a blueprint for success. It's a thought-out set of drawings and specifications that allows you to get the result exactly as you want, or better.

Imagine getting a fixed price building contract without architects' plans. Imagine being able to set a realistic time frame for the project or order the materials if you don't have any details on what it is you are building.

And yet...

This is exactly how many people approach their website developments:

- Asking for quotes about a redevelopment before finalizing what they want

- Providing the equivalent of just electrical engineer drawings to explain the entire house (technical & functional requirements)
- Providing the time frame up front before locking in the exact needs
- Choosing the builder without reviewing how they can deliver on the needs and wants
- Picking up a theme for one purpose and trying to squash it out as something completely different

The Solution

At all times through this process, imagine you are about to build your dream home or your next home, and you have experience in what didn't work previously or what wasn't quite right, but now you want to get that ideal home.

This time, you are going to work through the steps, plan out clearly and simply what it is you really need, and put you and your builders in the position to make smart decisions from the start.

This works for a simple 5-page advertorial or mini site as it does a large corporate 1,000-page site.

No plan = guess work

Let's go make a plan that gets you great results!

3

COMMON WEBSITE PLANNING MISTAKES.

L earning from the mistakes of others is better than going through them yourself.

Everyone makes mistakes when doing something new or if they don't have easy-to-use instructions. There are many areas in a web project where either side of the client/developer relationship can have issues. If you are more aware of them, hopefully you won't make those mistakes.

The first and most obvious mistake is not having any plan at all. Moving past that, most of the website planning mistakes listed are either in the selection stage of choosing who to work with, or in how you might make decisions that previously you would have considered "your brief".

Build a better plan by avoiding these traps.

Some stem from being overworked or time poor and taking the fast and lazy approach to writing a brief; others are because you just don't know any different.

This guide on how to make a better website brief is designed to help you avoid these traps. Read over them and see if you have done any before or are tempted to say or request one of them. Then with that in mind, work through the guide and you will understand why they aren't going to help you get a better result.

1. No Plan

The biggest single mistake you can make is to start the process of designing and building the site without a plan.

No plan = No method to get it right.

Even after nearly 20 years of helping people build web applications and sites, I still have conversations with individuals who haven't put together any plan at all.

If you want a better website, then you need a plan. Plain and straightforward!

Follow the steps in this Complete Website Planning Guide and you will have a plan that works!

2. Copy That Site

This is the easy way out. You see a site you "like the look of" and want your business to look like that.

You get your development team to copy it and they do, making it fit how your brand is represented. It looks pretty good, but it's just like selecting a theme and not applying any thought to what you need.

You have no idea if that site produces results. Many "good looking sites" might win awards but don't impact the business meaningfully.

It doesn't mean there is anything wrong with "copying" — many sites are of course copies of ideas seen elsewhere. Use other sites as inspiration and to help convey to your team what you want. If using a theme matches your budget and you can get the right website at the end of it, then that's a design and financial decision.

"Copy that site" isn't a website plan or brief.

---

3. I Want a Site Just Like (insert major brand here)

My favorite one of these is, "Make it look like Apple/Facebook only better".

Seriously, we hear this type of comment regularly. You aren't Apple or Facebook, so why would you want to copy them? Steve Jobs didn't get to create the products he did simply by copying other people.

Gather insight, ideas and intelligence from great sites. You don't even know if that 'great website' you are looking at actually performs. You can't see their analytics data or sales data.

Be realistic about your budget. These sites you dream to emulate probably have funds that might match significant portions of your business revenue. Unless you can spend that on the website, focus more on what you need.

4. I Have $X — What Can You Build For That?

Having a budget is, of course, imperative. So is knowing what you can afford to spend.

As any good business owner or marketing manager knows,

you first need to understand what you want, what it might cost and also what type of return it could bring you.

You might be able to afford to double what you propose to your developer if you knew it was going to help you get more business.

If you have a realistic plan and a budget, when you get quotes higher than what you can afford, you will be able to have a sensible conversation with developers on what they can take out that won't break everything now, and that can be added back later.

That is a better way. Also, maybe you just can't afford what you want or need. But that's a different conversation topic. Better you know up front before you start a project to find out it isn't what you need.

5. Stay Out Of the Ballpark

Oh no, not the ballpark!

Invariably we have all asked someone at some point in our lives, "Can you give me a ballpark cost for that?"

Except you won't ever again when seeking quotes for any other sites you are going to build.

Using our builder analogy, imagine expecting to get a realistic ballpark figure for a house with no drafts or plans. "I think I want a two-story three-bedroom house. Can you tell me how much?"

I would hope you wouldn't build a house like that, and I implore you to stop trying to get a price like that for a site you don't have any idea about.

If you have a scope or plan and want an estimate before a full fixed quote gets done, that's not unreasonable, but if you turn up with nothing but a number of rough pages, then you aren't going to get a brilliant result.

6. Can You Do Two Designs So We Can Choose a Developer?

Hopefully, most agencies or design teams would politely send you away at this point, but people still expect to get 'design' work done without payment or without giving a full briefing.

If you follow our guide, you will learn that visual design comes a long way down the path of planning a new site, and you also shouldn't expect to get quality design work done without it being part of the paid work.

Your ideas will be concise so that your design team will bring together one style you have already agreed on, rather than expecting to get multiple coherent designs knocked up as part of a pitch. Do the work to create an excellent brief, then you will find it easy to pick development teams and get great results.

7. Brief Briefs

An overly thin brief is one where you think you are giving useful information but are only providing a simple conversation outlining what areas of your site need to change.

For example, "We will want to change the About Us section, and we will give you new stuff later", or "We want the homepage to be different. If you can make it feel more modern that would work."

This isn't a brief. It might provide an overview that could be clarified, but it is way too 'brief' to be useful.

You will see why in later chapters.

8. Here's Our Old Site, Just Make It New

This is where you hand over a list of pages listed as if it's your sitemap with a few notes about how you want it to look like 'X' site.

A sitemap isn't just a list of the pages of your current site or a list of uncategorized URLs from a site scraper. A sitemap is part of the design of your site architecture and is a very important part of a good brief.

A scope or brief will include a form of sitemap like this, but it will provide a lot more information than just pages.

9. I Don't Want Much Content in It; No One Reads Content

As you review and understand what users want, you will see how important content, in all types, is for your business and marketing.

You also need to realize that in building your website for your business it is not about you and your opinions much at all. The biggest mistake many organizations make is building from the inside out rather than the outside in.

You will need content, high-quality content, and you will need to plan that content in advance. That's one part of how you will create an awesome website that works for your business.

These are just some of the mistakes you can make when planning a site.

The next chapters start the actual process of building your scope and turning it into a **Great Website Brief.**

4

WHAT RESULT DO YOU WANT FROM YOUR WEBSITE?

Many businesses will have several goals or objectives for their website. What are yours? How clearly explained are they? Does everyone know about them?

Steven Covey wrote in his book *The 7 Habits of Highly Effective People* about the need to begin with the end in mind. The *Habit* of knowing where you want to be when you reach the end before you take the first step.

For many businesses' (and life) practices, this is important and necessary to create a successful result or to know when you are there, that you have reached the end point.

In this chapter, I want to remind you about how important goals are for your website and your business so that you have a plan for success.

This chapter is an updated written version of a previous video I recorded on the subject. You can watch my **Goal Setting video** at your leisure (link: https://www.ireckon.com/design/goal-setting-website-scope/).

If you have no destination in mind, then any road is a good road.

Creating Your Success.

When creating your website brief/scope, you need to know exactly what success will look like.

It is pointless to run around your office high-fiving about winning a design award for your new website if that wasn't why you built it. The only celebrating should be about how it is meeting or exceeding the business goals you need for your business. Unless you are a design agency, then I doubt winning design awards is a real goal you have.

Why Focus So Much On Goals Up Front?

- They help you stay focused on what matters
- They help resolve conflicts
- They help guide difficult decisions
- When budget or other restrictions come into play, goals become very important in how you make hard calls on what stays or doesn't

Your website goals will guide every decision you make, every word you write, and will help guide the design team and development team in implementing something that works.

Goals for websites aren't overly complicated; there are only so many things your site can do for you.

It's not my role to tell you what the goals should be, you need to choose them, but here are some of the **key goals** you may end up choosing from:

- Leads/Inquiries

- Sales
- Customer Support engagement
- Phone calls
- Partial engagement (newsletter sign-ups, social likes, downloads, etc.)
- Reads/Ad views

If you had to pick just one, which one would it be?

One Goal To Rule Them All

In our blueprint method, we want you to create a hierarchy of goals so that you have an easy way to answer the most important questions when they arise.

You need to create a single 'Primary Goal'.

What specifically is the most important goal you want your website to achieve?

Don't fall into the trap of many websites where you want to make everything important and suffer from visual or process overload, or worse blandness and no clear and obvious essential elements.

Only you can truly answer this question. Make sure when you do you are very clear about it.

Goals That Work.

To help you with this, view our Website Goals Template and use it to get very clear on your primary goal.

Get your copy on the resources page here: https://ireck.in/wpgr

It is a free PDF template that you can use to help guide you through setting your goals.

You will notice on this template two essential elements:

1. Make your goals Specific, Measurable and Realistic
2. You can have additional goals

A goal isn't useful if you make it vague and generic.

e.g. "We want a modern and fresher feeling website that makes us look more hip."

There is nothing very particular about this, as it is entirely subjective. It offers nothing of measurable value to the business, and while I have heard this many times, it doesn't provide any value to you.

Instead something like, **"We want ten new inquiries a week for our premium products"** is specific and measurable. Make sure it's realistic too. If to date you only get ten inquiries every six months, and you don't have any supporting evidence about total market inquiries, then you might just set yourself up to be disappointed.

There is nothing like a stretch goal to get you to push forward in your market, but don't make it so unachievable it kills ambition in the site from the get go.

It could be, **"We want to get to six new inquiries every month, by month six, and then increase this once we have better data on our target market"**.

That sort of goal sets you up for success on many fronts, including a re-evaluation six months down the road.

If you haven't worked out your goals, then you aren't ready

to build a site that outperforms its competitors. Stop the guesswork and write out the goals now, so you have a clear pathway moving forward. When you have completed your site goals, move on to the next chapter.

5

WHO IS THE AUDIENCE FOR YOUR WEBSITE?

Who Is Your Focus?

One of the issues that many websites (and marketing efforts) have is a generic broad-brush approach of what they offer and whom their product should appeal to.

That will happen if you tend to have broad statements about who your audience is.

A typical response to the question, "Who is your audience?" is "Anyone who wants to buy my widget" etc.

That's super broad and not very helpful to focus your efforts on. Our goal throughout this entire series is to make your website work for you and be highly targeted. We want you building a result-orientated site.

Imagine telling your builder, "We just need about four bedrooms to fit all four of us." You are very likely to get four bedrooms, but how many bathrooms will you get, where will they be situated and what size are the rooms? That will all be left to chance or the builder's imagination.

Or more accurately, who is this website being built for?

Narrow Not Broad Focus.

To get a website that will get you highly focused results, you need to be able to focus in on your audience and list specifics that will match their needs.

You need to create a singular focus for a singular audience.

Your site (and business) might not just have one focus audience or product; you might sell clothes for men and women, and most companies do sell more than one thing. That just means you are going to need to do the audience identification task multiple times.

You don't want a site heavily focused on just one gender or type of clothing, so you need to make sure you understand each audience.

Note:

By now you will have noticed we talk about audiences not customers/clients in this section. Not all sites are about selling something, and not everybody buys the first time they come to your site.

When making a movie, for example, you are trying to appeal to a particular audience, and if you provide them what they like then they go away happy and continue to interact with you.

We want to treat our "ideal customers" as an audience. We want to prepare for them and understand them. We want to make sure we get them in our cinema, and they like what they are seeing and hearing. Then we can work on selling to them, but selling is only part of the puzzle. Let's get to know our audience first, before we count on them buying.

Who Are Your Actual Customers?

Identifying who your audience is starts with a general under-standing of your typical customers – those people who buy from you. Keep in mind that if you aren't selling to the right people at the moment, those you want to buy your product, then you need to be focusing on your ideal clientele, not the ones currently buying.

For the purpose of understanding your ideal customers, we will refer to them as your 'Jennies.' It's much easier when discussing people to use real people's names and to treat your target market as people, not things or abstract objects.

We will look at one singular Jenny to provide an example of how to understand and review your audience. You will most likely have multiple Jennies and many different needs for each Jenny, and you will give them all their own names.

Change Your Thinking.

It's not about what you want to sell to Jenny; you have to shift your thinking to understand **what Jenny wants.**

You might have a fantastic automated pool cleaner that you want to sell to Jenny, but focusing on the pool cleaner you have and not on Jenny's needs/wants will create for you a site filled with product pages, rather than a site designed around attracting Jenny and helping her solve a problem of hers.

You are going to want to build a persona (individual profile) for Jenny, as outlined in the 'What Jenny Wants' template.

Download: What   Jenny   Wants   PDF   Template
https://ireck.in/wpgr

Download: Example   WJW   Doc   Template
https://ireck.in/wpgr

Building Personas.

There are any number of extensive tools and methods for building detailed personas, and expanding on persona development as well as customer segmentation and research.

Don't get caught up in a perfect persona when you first start out.

You can end up in analysis paralysis over a problem that might not be as big as it needs to be.

What is most important throughout the process is you learning how important personas are and getting a better understanding of who your audience is.

Who's Your Jenny?

In identifying your Jenny, you need to understand a good summary of who she is, what the main problems are (relating to what you offer) and focused clarity on the problem/possible solutions.

Jenny might be a time-poor working professional, recently separated with several children and not loving the messy backyard.

The pool might be looking dirty and she has no interest or time to clean out all the leaves every week, and doesn't need the additional weekly expense of the pool man.

Her kids may be a little young to do this reliably. She is considering moving house to get rid of the pool and yard but is worried about more change for everyone at a difficult time.

If you extend your thinking to what solutions you have that

might appeal to Jenny, based on Jenny's problems, you are going to be looking at how to target her, what content and products might appeal to her, and where her thinking will be.

See how suddenly Jenny takes shape — she is now someone who can be related to.

The Different Focus.

Now you start to see how your entire development focus will change.

Previous Solution:

Generic page about automated pool cleaners.

Jenny Solution:

A focused page that targets time-poor people who don't need the hassle of cleaning their pool but want a pool.

More work? **Absolutely.**

Better result? **Absolutely!**

Once you have such focused content when you start marketing campaigns, you will be able to target ads to solve problems, the ideal method, supported by content and calls to action that will bring in better qualified people more ready to buy.

Underneath all this, would you still have a traditional catalog with products and a shopping cart? Most definitely. Instead of designing a site just about the product, we are developing a site for your ideal Jennies and helping them find their way through the site.

This is just an example of how understanding your audience works. Such knowledge is going to help you identify navigation, terminology and categorization throughout your site, content required, search optimization needs, artwork needed, color palettes and a whole lot more.

Apply It To Your Business.

For your business, you need to work through the process of getting very clear on who your audience/s are.

1. You start with a summary of them and then drill into the very specific focus areas for each type of audience.

If you were a **pub/bar in Sydney, Australia,** that is looking to better understand its audience, you might start by first creating some simple groups:

- Guys, Girls
- 25-40 year-olds
- Some sports interest and DJ music

2. From there you need to make that a little more specific.

If you only show two types of sport in the bar, then appealing to all sports lovers is a long stretch. If your sports bar area shows as many sports as you can, then you are going to break sports interests into all the types you are currently showing or wanting to promote in your bar:

- NFL
- NBA
- Rugby Union (and the different competitions you show)
- Rugby League
- AFL
- Tennis
- Formula 1

3. Now you are going to start identifying your Jennies.

In this instance, you have both Jennies and Jims.

Jim:

- 25-ish
- Tradesman
- Has a partner — both like to come out together or individually
- Big league fan, but likes most sports
- Likes to see but not hear all the sports action — prefers being there with friends chatting while watching games in the background

Jenny:

- 24
- Working young professional
- Loves NFL (member of her club team and goes to live games)
- Lives alone and doesn't like watching TV games on her own
- Likes to meet a couple of friends and watch and listen to games at the pub on Saturdays
- Goes out later elsewhere

In each instance, you can build up a profile of the types of people that frequent your business, or who you want to frequent your business, and should be able to see already how your marketing messages and approach currently do or don't appeal to this audience.

As you build it, the questions you should have started forming in your mind are:

- How well do we cater for them in our bar?

- What do we do that attracts them and makes them want to come back?
- What type of web content and stories will we need to appeal to this person?
- What offer would best appeal to them?
- What would they do if they came to our website looking to see if we have something that appeals to them?
- And many others like them

You should be able to see why understanding your audience is one of the primary key platforms of building any great new site.

For example, if you have a law practice, you could rebuild your site focused on what your services are and what you want to tell people you do, or you can build your site around the people, problems and *solutions* you can help provide.

Ultimately, as mentioned at the beginning of this chapter, it's about changing your focus. You are changing your focus from a 'me-centric' internal view of what you offer, to a customer-focused view where you seek to understand who your offer best suits and what their needs are.

We know which one is a more robust method.

Write down the audiences you serve and build as many personas as you can for your ideal customers. Then move on to the next chapter.

6

WHAT ARE THE MUST-HAVES FOR YOUR WEBSITE?

K nowing what things you absolutely must have for your business to work correctly is as important as everything else we have covered so far.

No Compromise.

Unless you have an unlimited budget for your next web project (note: if you do, please call as we'd love to help), the result you get will most likely have some forms of compromise from your ideal wish list.

Compromises can take several forms, including purely budgetary considerations as well as the level of work required, or "it seemed like a good idea at the time" but on reflection doesn't make sense.

What you mustn't compromise on is the things your business MUST HAVE.

To Be Included.

In setting your primary and secondary goals for your site,

you should have a very clear understanding of what you are trying to achieve and what success looks like.

Often though there are business MUST-HAVES that don't necessarily figure into the primary goal directly but which are important to your business long term.

These MUST-HAVES are something you need to outline in your scope and make sure everyone involved in the project fully understands their importance.

Your primary goal for this web build might be to increase Leads and Sales. These invariably will have some other marketing sub-goals attached, which might include email address collection via newsletter sign ups or other forms that fit into your marketing channel.

Your customer service team may also need a robust and healthy FAQ/Q&A area supported by a ticketing system for support requests. While important to them this may not get listed or scoped until very late in the process after important decisions have already been made.

These MUST-HAVES can often highlight back of house functions that are critical to business processes flowing smoothly.

You might need real-time communication with a third-party Inventory Management system for your e-commerce store or a particular multi-step email notification pathway including integration with your shipping provider. If these remain as afterthoughts, then the wrong choices in the scope can be made, and not enough questions will be asked early enough to see them fit nicely into the overall site.

Attention to Detail.

Initially, it is all the highest pages and the shiniest elements that get attention first, and as the budget gets consumed and the energy for the project dwindles, items last in the development list get generic implementations or left until stage 2/3.

Use our MUST-HAVEs list builder to gather the essential items your business must have in this website development. This list will become a critical part of the introduction to your scope and as you work through the next sections you will see how you can introduce it into the scope.

Download our Template: https://ireck.in/wpgr

Don't be worried if you do an initial draft to get started so you can keep moving through the process. While you work on the later stages, share the MUST-HAVEs list with other team members to get their additions or comments, and then implement that back into the other work you have done.

Don't forget heads of departments for areas you mightn't consider as part of the web build. You will often learn how they would appreciate the site to do 'X' early enough in the process that you can solve their biggest headaches.

When the Must-Haves list has been completed, move to the next chapter.

7

RESEARCH

Getting Started.

Chapters 3 to 5 were very much about you uncovering your needs in more detail and starting on the path of determining who you are building this website for. This chapter is the introduction into expanding your knowledge about your audience. It's about moving away from gut assumptions, generalizations, and manager-driven opinion to using research to gain knowledge and data that can drive sensible decision making.

In-depth research is a skill that can require lots of experience and resources. Our goal here is to give you the starting points that allow you to become proficient in a solid introductory research process for any project in keeping with the overall objective of this guide, which is for organizations that don't have all the resources but still need to improve their processes and results. Use these options and you will be acquiring useful and intelligent information that will help you make better decisions. You can always learn more and engage specialists as your business processes mature.

Understand The Needs Of Your Audience.

In Chapter 4 we looked at your audience and gaining an understanding of them, which highlighted an approach focused on getting a better idea of who your ideal customers are.

You can base it on existing customers whom you wish to replicate or those people you know you want as customers.

To build a website designed to not only attract your ideal clients but to also convert them, requires you to understand their needs, wants, and desires.

If you have learned one thing so far in this guide, it should be that 'it's all about the customer.' To make sure we can put ourselves in the minds of our clients and see it from their perspective, we need to research more about them and how they go about finding answers to their questions, and what triggers them to take action.

Research isn't just making an assumption from one view of a single piece of evidence, it is about gathering as much available information on the topic as you can to help guide your decisions through the rest of the process.

As Erika Hall wrote in *Just Enough Research*:
"Research is simply systematic inquiry. You are solving the problem of a lack of information."

Make it practical as well. If you are starting out with a small site and don't have any or many customers, then you will probably be unable to get much existing research data, but can ask prospects or ideal targets to gather their perspective. Then continue the research process post launch to better understand and improve what you built.

Learn From What You Already Have.

The starting point for any research on your website development should be your current site. Instead of making snap 'gut feel' decisions about what you need, learn to use data. Many reasons for a website change often come from internal boredom with the current site or frustration with how it's managed.

While it's true that having a site that's hard to administer will make life harder for you, if the site is working well for your customers you need to be very careful about why you are proposing to change it and what needs to change.

You will want to start looking through your analytics (e.g. Google Analytics or similar programs) and getting a better understanding of what your current site performance is.

If you don't have access to or are not even sure if you have Google Analytics (the most common free analytics tool) on your site, there is a simple check you can make:

- Go to your website
- In your browser, right-click on the home page
- Choose 'View page source' – this will bring up the HTML for the page you are on
- Choose CTRL-F (win) or COMMAND-F (Mac) to bring up the Find panel
- Type in: Analytics or UA-
- If the code exists on your site, it will highlight a code with a value similar to this: **UA-159492-3**
- If no results show up for either of those searches, then it is highly unlikely you have Google Analytics on the site

What To Do If There Are No Analytics:

- Get in contact with whoever controls the current site content and coordinate with them to get analytics on the site
- Once added, you are going to need to let it gather data for a month or more. The more data, the better any observations
- Move on to other parts of your research and scope, then come back to check your decisions when you have enough data to work with

What To Do If There Are Analytics:

- Get in contact with whoever built or managed the site before you and ask who has the analytics access
- Get yourself added to it as an Admin
- Once inside you need to start learning what data matters and what doesn't

Just because you have analytics installed doesn't mean it will be well configured or providing you with the best insights.

With the new goals in mind, you can start to analyze what currently assists those goals and what is missing.

Ultimately, you want to know what parts of your site and from what source (referral site or engine) lead to the most conversions that matter to your business.

The key things you will start with:

1. Traffic sources (which ones currently matter most to your business)
2. Content performance (what pages/content seem to hold people on your site and lead to the most conversions)

3. Goals/Conversion (are you tracking these correctly and what do they tell you e.g. Inquiries, sales, etc).

Understanding analytics and the many threads of information it can provide you is beyond the scope of what our guide is here to teach. There are many articles, guides, and courses online that will help you get your analytics working correctly, inform and educate you on key metrics, and help you use it in making better decisions.

Key research topics within your analytics:

- Gaps in your current content to what your customer analysis identifies
- Problematic pages that users bounce off and which don't help them
- What your goals are and which ones you can measure
- Gaps in traffic sources.

Learn About Behavior.

User behavior data on your site is the best way to win over anyone in your organization that hasn't switched to a data-focused approach to your development. When you are looking to understand site flows for information architecture fixes or conversion problems, there is no better way than to watch and learn than from Usability Testing Tools.

Listed below are several methods that will help you better understand how people are currently utilizing your site. This type of information will help you make more informed decisions. Note that this practice should be included on your new site to ensure the latest work you complete achieves the goals you set out to make. Always Testing!

Usability Tests:

1. Heatmaps

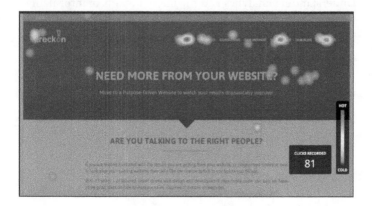

Heatmaps are graphical depictions of users using a page on your site. They normally highlight clicks, movement, and scrolling on a given page. From reviewing heatmaps, you can determine patterns on how current users are utilizing the site. Many heatmap tools will also separate these maps into device specific maps.

2. Screen Recordings

Screen Recordings show real people using your site, including where they click and the pages they visit. These recordings allow you to sit as if looking over the shoulder of a user and experience what they are experiencing. What they can't tell you is the user's intent or thinking, but they show a lot of what they do, which helps you gain useful information about how your current site gets used.

3. Form Analytics

Form Analytics are particularly helpful in highlighting problems with forms on your site. You get to see which fields cause users to slow down or reconsider their engagement, and where they drop off in a form. This type of data is a must when improving your existing site and even more so when you design fresh forms for the goals in your new site.

4. Funnel Analysis

Funnel Analysis works like Form Analytics and Form Analysis in Google Analytics and is very useful in understanding how users travel through your site on their pathway to completing a key goal. Analysis like this is invaluable in understanding e-commerce sites and where site users drop out of your intended pathway to a sale/conversion. The analysis will show you how many people are leaving your funnel and at what point. With linked recordings and heatmaps you can understand much more about why they are leaving this process, which will help you design a better path.

5. User Testing

User Testing is the step from hidden passive testing to more active forms of testing. You can utilize online resources or bring in people to use your site and complete several predetermined tasks. You observe what they do, hear what they are thinking and expressing, and seek to understand how they interpret the content, signals, and options on your site. With the ability to get actual feedback, you get third-party validation of what is happening and acquire more knowledge to fix any problems.

The first four items in this list you can get using online app providers such as Crazy Egg, Inspectlet, Hotjar or others. You would sign up and pay to use their tools, have a small piece of Javascript code added to your site by your current development team, and then within minutes you will have data to start analyzing and visualizing.

It's incredibly powerful and an important start to learning more about what is currently happening, and once you have rolled out your new project it's part of your ongoing regular analysis of what's occurring on the site.

* * *

Ask Questions.

One of the oldest and most accurate ways to gather useful information is to ask questions of real people – interviews.

When you have data that helps you spot patterns or highlights areas you don't understand about what your clients might want or need, or more importantly why they are behaving in a certain way on your existing site, you can ask people directly.

There are multiple ways to get direct feedback. The simplest is to get on the phone and talk to someone, or visit them in their environment and find out what matters most to them.

This process of direct feedback can be used in smaller ongoing changes as well as in research for a new project.

Let's say you have modified a client payment screen for invoices from your company – you could ensure you get copied into all notifications and then contact each client to get immediate feedback on the changes.

When you do a direct survey with a client, make sure you stick to the primary elements you want feedback on. In this example you could ask:

- Did you notice the payment pages had changed?
- Were the options easy to understand?
- Do you think this page is better than the previous one? (if they have used the previous one)

- Why?

Make these calls within minutes of the payment arriving, so it is top of mind for the user. You will get direct and priceless feedback from them, and it shows you care about what you are offering as well.

If conducting less specific research in interviews, you will ask questions that don't direct the answers but seek to gather honest answers to the type of problems they have, and have them outline what a solution would look like to them.

Instead of asking, "Do you use the local Snap Fitness Centre?" you could be asking, "What types of exercise do you do?" and "Is any of that in an organized environment?"

In this type of qualitative research, you are aiming to uncover information that provides insight into bigger questions than how an existing customer used a process.

Not all scenarios would make such direct surveying practical, as transactions occur at any time of the day and across many time zones.

Using Web-based tools to ask questions.

You can direct visitors to your site questions using a variety of methods.

Most polling/survey tools for web studies will provide one of these options:

- Link to a questionnaire
- Pop-up panel or box that has either the question or a call to action to participate
- Sidebar or footer-style direct questions

There are other types of options but utilizing one of these will give you enough information to assist.

The types of questions you can ask depends on the information you are trying to gather.

Some tools like Hotjar will allow you to poll a single question to specific pages. You can ask people on a product page whether the information on the page answers the questions they have about your product, and if it doesn't what would they like added to the page.

If you don't currently have the audience you are after, you can contact other site owners and look to conduct a survey of their users/clients who are your ideal market segment.

Turning Research into Useful Information.

Now that you have gathered a lot of ideas, information, and data, it's time to start planning how to deliver it in a useful, user-friendly method that will help meet your goals.

By moving away from assumptions to compiling common themes into stories and answers about your ideal audience and clients, you will be able to complete more detailed personas and have a list of common problems, possible conceptual solutions, and lists of ideas that can be refined into something practical for the actual development phases.

Sorting Your Data.

After completing your research, you will need to sort the data you have gathered so it can be used effectively. One of the easiest and most common ways to sort the collected data into useful information is to compile an 'Affinity Diagram'.

An affinity diagram is simply data listed in themes or groups.

The offline method for creating affinity diagrams is to use Post-it notes and a whiteboard. You write down every idea/piece of data onto individual Post-it notes and then these can be visually sorted into 'columns' or groups on the whiteboard.

There are also numerous tools you can use online to make an affinity diagram; one of the easiest is Trello, which is the tool used in the screen shots below. In Trello terms, a 'List' = 'Group/Theme' and a 'Tile' = 'Card/Post-it'.

In each instance, you are trying to create functional groupings that will help you better understand what you are trying to design.

One diagram might focus on user observations and thinking whereas another might be more concerned with usability and visual design.

You will use the information gathered in numerous ways. Some of it will help you build better personas, others will stand out as obvious content categories, but all of it should help you determine what you need to bring together for your new site to help your audience get a better result from what you provide them.

Using Trello as an example.

Gather all your notes and summaries from interviews, polls, user surveys, your internal customer and sales teams, and have it ready to group together. You can do this as a group (ideally) or, if you are the sole resource, on your own.

- Create a new Trello board
- Create a first list (column) called Legend, which you can use to help identify what colors you are using
- Create individual tiles for types of data or interviews, etc. Give each a unique color
- Create a list to add tiles (I called this one 'Ungrouped' in this instance)

- Start adding information you have gathered from your interviews. Try to keep the title as succinct as possible. If necessary add more data inside the tile
- Add color labels to each tile to represent where this observation or comment was gathered from. It's easy to see common items this way

Affinity Diagram in Trello

Once you have added a good number of tiles, the list will start to become a bit unmanageable, and you will want to add your groups so you can drag tiles into them and start the process of grouping.

You may already have groups in your mind from your reviews of the data, or quite possibly they will stand out from the data you are adding in.

Note: If doing this with Post-it notes offline it's very much the same process.

In our example of a legal company with data gathered from interviewing young couples and families about wills, you could end up with group headings like:

Lack of Knowledge, Fear of Legal Process/Lawyers, Money

You can add these as lists in Trello.

Then it's simply a matter of dragging related tiles into the most appropriate column.

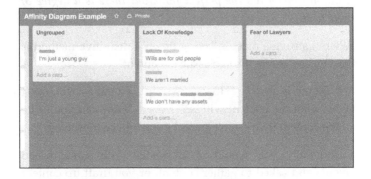

Using affinity diagrams/tools is going to help you create useful information lists that help you solve issues and plan better as you progress to the next stages.

Not all data you gather will fit neatly into a list or group, but it is still crucial. An observations document that records items of high relevance to your project will allow you not to forget comments or observations of behavior that will impact design or other functional items.

For example, noticing that everyone gets a very slow page load on a particular part of an existing site (or all of it) should get you to record, "Current site is very slow and leads to user frustration or abandonment." You would then add to your design scope, "Site needs to load faster (under 'X' seconds) on any (or listed) devices."

From Data to Design.

The next four chapters (Sitemaps, Page Scoping, Wire-framing, and Content) are listed in the order that seems to make the most sense in a linear process.

In reality, the process is more concurrent than linear, where elements you work on affect items in another part of this process and you need to adjust in each area.

It doesn't mean it's the perfect flow, but there is a degree of logic to it.

Where I struggle most in laying down a definitive method is the 'chicken before the egg' issue of content.

The debate is always, "How can you plan a page if you don't know what the content will be?" versus "How can you write all the content if you don't know how it will be presented?"

Traditionally, you would be presented with some design layouts and asked to gather content, or you draft up content for the designer who then wedges that into the theme they have already chosen for your site.

Neither of these methods creates the right result but in the absence of a better method what else can you do?

Depending on each project, I work almost in parallel through the next four steps. With the core content needs recognized, but not written, I understand the topics, the goal and aim for that content, and what its purpose is.

I would then step through Chapter 7 (Sitemap) and Chapter 8 (Scope) to define everything about the needed pages. I would usually then have enough to request the initial content because the scope would have outlined content needs pretty well.

Everyone needs to understand that nothing is final at this point, but it's OK. Once the wireframing has been done and approved (Chapter 9), when we get to Chapter 10 (Content is King) we should be able to direct the final content drafts with the specific visual elements needed.

Thus, if we want a call-out panel on a particular piece of content that might not be written yet but the bulk of the page content is, we can now request from the content team that particular element with more accurate requirements e.g. a suggested link, purpose, etc.

This is true for visual content requirements as well – we discuss this more in Chapter 10.

* * *

Note about the rest of the book:

Moving forward, each of the following chapters exists in conjunction with the next, and you will most likely be updating in each of the areas as you refine your scope.

8

DRAFTING A MAP

Drafting a Website Sitemap.

C reating a visual sitemap helps everyone involved see the scope of the project and helps to get people discussing the project at a macro level in one or two pages.

What Is a Sitemap?

A sitemap is a list of pages of a website. There are several meanings for the term site map:

- In Web Design, it means pages organized in a document showing their hierarchy and structure to help with the planning process
- In Website Management it refers to a HTML page on the site that lists the pages of the site in a hierarchical format to help users find pages within the site
- In Search Engine Optimization (and others) it means a structured XML format document that tells search engines about the pages of the site, their relationships, and where to find them

For this planning phase of your website, it is the first type we are referring to. Typically, it will be a visual diagram.

Why Use A Sitemap?

One of the key roles a sitemap has to offer is to help everyone involved in the project, especially your main stakeholders, have a simplistic way to gauge the size and scope of what is being undertaken.

When trying to plan how to achieve goals, establish where your must-haves fit in, how much content you will need and what other resources will be required, and how to get the necessary budget, having a way to provide size, scale, and purpose in a simple one- or two-page document is critical.

Not everyone in the decision-making process wants to read through pages of specifications and field lists. Many want to know the macro level, coupled with some other critical questions, so they feel they understand what is being proposed.

If you think about a list of directions compared to the actual route drawn on the map, one is used to get an overall picture of how, while the other is applied in the detail of what you need to do at any given moment. The sitemap summarizes at the top level the project and key elements – it's the zoomed-in view of the new site.

It is also a great preliminary checklist and way to get initial thoughts on paper to build from.

How To Draw a Sitemap.

There are a couple of ways to draft a sitemap, either as a simple list or as a flow chart (diagram).

Which method you choose might be determined by how you best work, and in many ways both have a role to play in identifying the types of pages and areas of your site you are going to need.

You will find it easier to start creating the top level as a chart and then, depending on the depth of the site, progressing to a list, before producing a final set of flow charts.

Let's step through how these work.

For this example of how to chart a sitemap we will use **http://draw.io** (a web-based diagram app).

Start Your Sitemap.

Let's work through the sitemap for a hypothetical legal practice.

- Open the app and choose a method for saving your files. Typically we would use Dropbox. The app can't update files if you choose the **Device** option and it can be annoying to save many copies – Dropbox manages all this nicely.
- Select **Create New Diagram**

Note: In the examples shown, we are working in a simplistic way to connect information we know we want to have on our site, and translate that into our sitemap and scope. There are many expanded and advanced areas that can be covered in choosing the information architecture and other needs. In this example, we want to provide a practical how-to for everyone, rather than just advanced practitioners.

Background

Our legal practice looks after both personal law and commercial law. It's a location-based practice with a team of 20 and covers a broad range of each legal service.

This summary of our business gives us some basic product/content groupings. We also have a pretty good idea about some fundamental pages most companies would need, for example, a Contact and Locations page, some form of About Us company page, and legal docs e.g. privacy policy etc.

For many companies, starting a sitemap will begin like this. It's a starting point that helps you group what you already know, which can then be improved on and expanded step by step as we move through the process.

It's much easier to see what needs improvement when you have it laid out in front of everyone.

Let's lay these pages down in our charting software to help us visualize what we are working with:

- First, make sure you have selected **Landscape** in the **Paper Size** options in the right-hand column
- Drag in the rectangular boxes from the left-hand objects panel
- Type the name of the box. Do this for all the pages you are going to add now

Your starting sitemap will look a little like this:

Don't bother connecting the boxes yet (with lines and arrows), as you will probably end up changing your mind a few times about what pages live where, and the hardest thing to do is these connections, so leave them until last.

In advanced sessions, this process might be done with Post-it notes in a meeting room, which allows you to build out all the pages and shuffle them until everyone agrees, then create the sitemap. Pen and paper work well, too.

The Obvious.

Knock over all the super easy stuff up front as well i.e. the pages you are relatively sure will need to be on the site based on your current site or competitors', or what you know to be good practice.

Once you see the sitemap built out you will be able to determine what pages still make sense and keep them, modify them or remove them quickly later in the design process.

Try to remember that when looking at your existing site and other people's sites it isn't about copying, it's about getting ideas to make decisions from. Always ask 'what's the purpose' for every page you add.

We want you to be thinking through the 'best' structure for your new site, not just re-skinning what you already have (see common mistakes).

So, with the extra pages on our site now added, the next version would start to look a little like this:

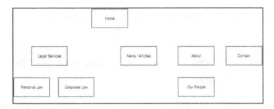

Easy so far.

That's quite typical of how you would start drafting a new site.

Expanding Your Offering.

As we break down the legal services that we offer, they can be added to the sitemap as subpages under Legal Services.

As an example:

These outline the topics or subcategories of our services.

They match up pretty well to the content we already have in online and offline documents, and importantly are the subject matter areas we offer to our clients.

Ultimately, this is the offer we believe we have that we present to our prospective and current clients.

At this point, we aren't sure how much content we will have per topic area, and it's possible, as we continue through our planning process, that some topics will end up with additional content.

For example, we aren't sure if the Family Law page might have subpages for Divorce, Pre-Nuptials, and Child Custody or whether this will all live on the one page.

We may not know this entirely until after the research phases are finished and content discussions finalized.

At this point, we are trying to cover all the key base pages/topics we know we need.

We haven't dug deep into content architecture, depth of content topics or other related information needs.

We will address these progressively through the following stages of our scope.

This phase is about learning how to create the basic sitemap and update it incrementally through the process until we can create the final sitemap version.

Here is the initial sitemap that we will use in the next stage of our scoping process:

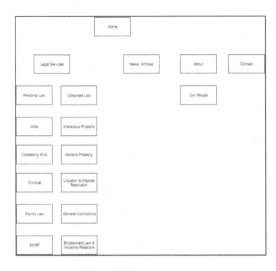

Below is an example of how this would look if you choose to do it in more of a list format using something like Excel (or Google Sheets).

There are some other final steps we need to take to finish off a sitemap. These steps tie in with the next steps in our scoping process, so we will complete the numbering and connecting steps once we are sure everything has been added.

9

SCOPE IT OUT

Scope Out The Pages of Your Website.

I t is time to write up what the purpose is of each and every page on your site, and outline clearly what you expect to be on each page.

Drafting Out the Website Scope

On your first run through of the page scope, it will definitely be a draft. The scoping process should be progressive and will require you to gather specifics you don't know when you first start writing it.

That's a normal part of the process.

During this phase, your goal is to uncover all the relevant information that will help everyone involved in your project do their jobs more easily and to detail what you want with a lot of clarity.

Note: You do not need to be technically orientated to write the scope. You just need to be able to think and be observant.

Linked at the bottom of this chapter are a single-page template and also a Google Sheet example of the type of scoping document I regularly use in preparing comprehensive/briefed sites.

The purpose of providing this template isn't to say "this is the only way to do it". However, the most common question I get asked when I request a proper brief from a prospective client is, "Do you have an example I can fill in?"

The template is an example and yes it can get filled in, and these instructions will explain how. You can create your own format and use that; the layout just needs to be consistent for the entire brief and achieve the same, or similar, result.

Start With The Sitemap.

The sitemap is an easy first step and it gives an outline to the project. It helps to speed this part up, as the initial pages are already marked out and grouped.

As you progress through this stage, you will find the process is now dynamic meaning things will be changing here and on the sitemap, as you will no doubt identify pages that aren't yet in the sitemap.

Once you then add them to the sitemap, you will need to scope them here, which is great as it means the process is working – we are uncovering needed items that make up your site.

While working through our sitemap, we will create little scoping briefs for each page no matter how small.

The Website Scoping Template.

Here is what the Google Sheets template looks like:

1.0	Page	
	URL	*optional*
Summary of page / Goal		
This should clearly articulate the goal of this page, and any sub-goals. What is this page here to do?		
Functionality		
As much information about things that need to happen on this page.		
Media / Copy Requirements		
List of items required, a bullet list is fine.		
Amendments		
Date	Who	What

Note about the Numbering

In the top left of the template example, you will see a number '1.0,' which signifies the page number in our sitemap.

The numbering is structured to help visualize the navigation quickly as well as information architecture (the structure of all the content and information of the site).

e.g. If Personal Law is 2.0, then Wills underneath it would be 2.1, etc.

For now, leave the numbering until later in the process, it saves you a lot of moving/renumbering time later on.

The Example.

Look back at our legal services sitemap and we will pick our way through it page by page to scope out the entire site.

The Home Page will be our 1.0 page. That's our main page and can't be forgotten –though this most likely won't get written up until we have completed everything else about the site. Working in this way is opposite to a lot of planning approaches that aim to solve the Home Page first.

Typically, I prefer this approach, where we scope out all of the pages from the bottom upwards and finish at the top.

This ensures I have thought through what experience I want to create before I worry too much about the gateway.

It also means I have clarified my site priorities as well, and that helps me identify the most important elements needed on the Home Page.

First Steps.

For this example, let's write up the Contact Page first.

Note: Don't worry about getting it 100% accurate, you are most likely going to change your mind as you work through this process.

You may want to modify elements as you practice digging deeper into the page-by-page needs and that's what we want.

It's much easier to clarify and change here in notes than it is once actual development has started.

In the Google Sheet follow these steps:

- Click the arrow to the right of the Template tab (bottom of the screen) and the following menu will appear:

- Now click **Duplicate** and a new tab will be added. You can see I already added one for **Home Page**
- The new tab will turn up between the Template tab and the Home Page tab
- **Click and hold** it and move it to the right of Home Page
- **Click the arrow** on the new tab and choose **Rename**, change it to **Contact**

Note: This process can be followed for every page you add. Make sure you keep them in the order of your sitemap. Like anything in an organizational tree, keeping it all in order helps you see if you have covered everything and then easily find what you need when going back to edit.

Fill In The Page Scope.

Now we will start to put content into the template. I would usually delete the page number if I don't know what it is going to be yet, or change it to 'XX' so I can do a search across everything later, looking for all instances of 'XX' to fix up.

Elements to fill in

Page: The name of the page.

Note: This isn't the title of the page that is displayed on the site; this is purely the identification of the page in relation to the sitemap and its function. In the content phase, these titles for display will be clarified and finalized ready for use in production.

URL: The file path on the final website e.g. /contact/ or /contact-us/

Note: You can leave these at this point unless you are well versed in the URL structure you want. It might well be that this gets left to your online marketing or SEO team, depending on the people in your project team and what you uncover in the research phase.

Summary of page/Goal: A clear explanation of what the heck this page is doing here on your site! Why/what should it be doing? The purpose of the page.

Note: You might not know the answer to this. Brilliant! Now we start to get to the pointy end of understanding what you learned about your audience and what you think you need, and finding if the basic 'copy that' plan has legs. Why spend money and energy making pages on a site if they serve no purpose? Would you print thousands of brochures for no reason?

Think back to the **goal setting** chapter and reflect on the overall goals for your site. How does this page support them?

For example, "Make it easy for our prospective clients to reach us in multiple ways."

That gives you something to work with.

Ideally it's specific, measurable, and realistic.

Functionality: This should be a list of everything you need on this page.

Note: It doesn't have to be the technical description of 'how' things will happen. For complex business flows, we will add those into additional areas later. It also isn't specific content. On our Contact Page, we would list 'Phone number' but we wouldn't list the specific phone number to use. That's content and comes in the content guide.

I would prefer bullet points for this list, but unfortunately Google Sheets doesn't like bullet formatting inside cells, so I just insert new lines for each point.

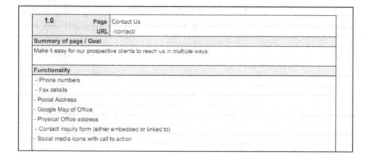

The importance of the functionality elements cannot be overstated.

Don't get hung up on the exact 'how' at this point. The goal is to get the detail onto paper so it can be seen.

I cheated previously and added 'Inquiry Form' into the sitemap, based on my experience. However at the sitemap phase that might never have occurred to you.

As you write this out, you should be evaluating your current site for what might be necessary, and also other websites that appear to offer the kind of experience you want your customers to have.

In doing so, you notice the form and then add it to your list.

By not worrying about the specific content, your focus remains on what you want and need without being overly concerned if you put the right content in place. This method will eliminate the necessity to have complete, final content in this phase. That might not even be your job, so you may have to delay the scope finalization to get the perfect copy. Trust me, that could be a long time coming.

When adding 'inquiry form' to the requirements, hopefully it will then trigger questions about where does that inquiry go? What happens next?

Let's say you go and investigate, or reflect on the last inquiry you made online. What happened? Did you get a response on screen? Was there an email sent to you? Etc.

Now that you have thought through what you want to happen, you need to add additional functionality to cater for this.

Let's say we have decided to have a separate form (as per the example sitemap) that isn't embedded, this means an extra page is needed.

If the inquiry form then loads a new page for the Thank You screen, this also needs to be noted in not only the sitemap but in each of the scope pages.

First, let's finish off this page.

Media/Copy Requirements:

List here the items you will need to complete this page.

Note: If you have specific artwork or copy that you think this page will need, list it out. Again you don't need the specific files; this is for later in the process of gathering content assets.

Examples might be:

- 1800 phone number plus the local (international dial) number
- Determine who will receive the inquiries (need email address/s)
- Clear icons for Facebook and Twitter
- Photo of our building could look good on this page.

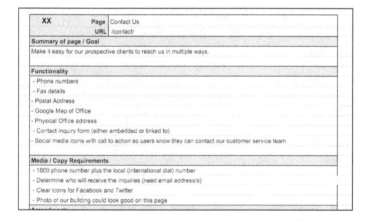

XX	Page	Contact Us
	URL	/contact/
Summary of page / Goal		
Make it easy for our prospective clients to reach us in multiple ways.		
Functionality		
- Phone numbers		
- Fax details		
- Postal Address		
- Google Map of Office		
- Physical Office address		
- Contact inquiry form (either embedded or linked to)		
- Social media icons with call to action so users know they can contact our customer service team		
Media / Copy Requirements		
- 1800 phone number plus the local (international dial) number		
- Determine who will receive the inquiries (need email address/s)		
- Clear icons for Facebook and Twitter		
- Photo of our building could look good on this page		

Amendments: Used once you start finalizing the document and sharing it with your team.

Note: This also allows for scope amendments and changes to occur when working with your developers, and for them to be recorded – useful for testing and understanding what changes have occurred to the original, and also if there are cost implications.

The beauty of Google Sheets is that the entire process can be viewed transparently by all and easily shared, and version control is inbuilt.

This is the updated sitemap including our new Inquiry Form page:

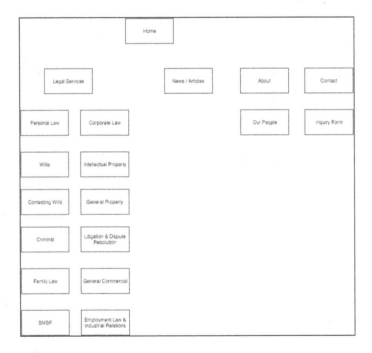

New Worksheets.

Let's now create two new worksheets for the Inquiry Form and the Inquiry Response pages, using the duplicate method that we used above.

In the new Inquiry Form worksheet, we will follow the same process to outline what we want.

Note:

In this worksheet we are going to be more definitive. It is a functional element, not just a general page, which will ultimately need very specific requirements.

It's OK to start with basics for some pages, but before the end of the process you will need to make sure you have worked out the exact requirements for every page and all functional elements.

Page Goal:
To make it super easy for prospective clients to inform us of their needs or questions, and to help existing clients contact us if they need help.

Functionality:
Here list out the fields you will want in your contact form. What information do you know you want to gather?

Answer this question first:
If you open up your email in the morning and have a new client inquiry, what would it say?

Then ask:
How can I get the answers above in the simplest possible way from a user?

Fill in the fields in the sheet.

Here's an example:

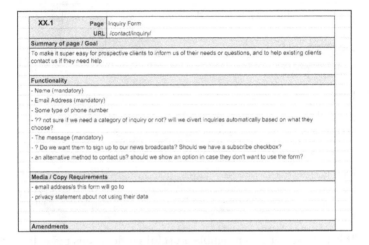

I specifically left out something important to emphasize what steps you need to take.

We have determined it is going to go to a thank you page and yet there's no mention of that in this document yet. It's important that you link up every decision you make, so it is clear where it needs to be.

Which also highlights needing information about automated emails:

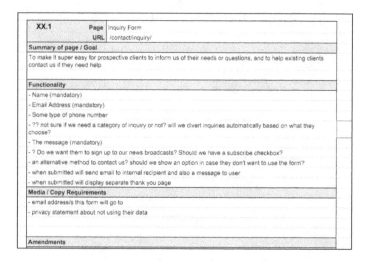

It is now starting to resemble a useful guide to this page. It's not an afterthought late in the design or development process, and shouldn't be. Getting the 'inquiry' could or should be your primary goal for the site, so focusing on the actual page that does the converting is more important in many ways than the pages before it.

Let's Do That Again.

Next, let's also do the thank you page.

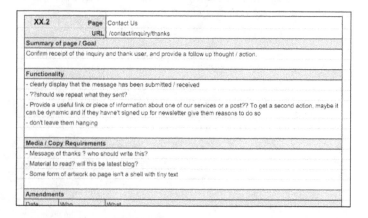

As you work your way through this process, you should be able to add in more bits of information.

As you open this up to help from other team members, they too will be able to add in important pieces of information that will be critical to getting this right.

Yes, not everything can be decided by you or up front, hence the use of '??' – or a similar notation.

It can be something you use to go back through and clarify what is going to be needed.

In looking at this functionality, you need to come back to the understanding of how this will work for the person using it, not always about what you want out of it.

For example, when you look at the way to add additional content on the thank you page, you need to balance between cluttering the screen and the person seeing it not being able to clearly see the key objective – confirmation of their inquiry – and also whether adding something extra adds value to them.

If someone has made an inquiry on our development site about a possible new project, linking out to a chapter in this guide makes sense for them, if they haven't seen it – especially a chapter about choosing your developer.

Here we give them tools to help them in their choice and not necessarily another post from our blog, which might be contextually irrelevant to them at this point.

It might not seem that important to go down to the next level of detail.

However if you don't, then this might not be included in the core project budget/estimation, and might not be part of your content team's production requirements.

Getting In Depth.

There are business processes that will also need matching to this as well, and if you don't have them in your project plan, they will most likely be forgotten.

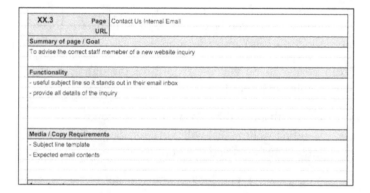

And, more importantly, the one that goes to the person making the inquiry.

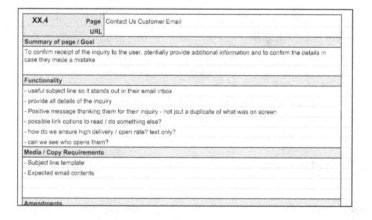

That's the starting point for building out the actual page-by-page scope. And it does need to be page by page. As much as you would love to lump every page into a common template and guide, if you are going to do that you might as well get a simple out-of-the-box WordPress theme with a right sidebar and just make every page the same.

Content Page Example.

If you are still here, then you follow on with the process of determining the purpose of every page. What role does it serve your customers, why does it belong on the site, and how will it fulfill that role?

Let's do the Legal Services Page.

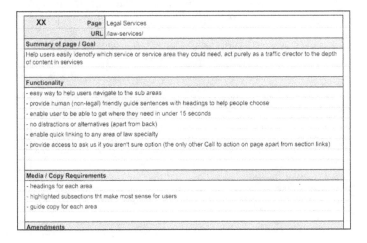

XX	**Page**	Legal Services
	URL	/law-services/

Summary of page / Goal

Help users easily idenotfy which service or service area they could need, act purely as a traffic director to the depth of content in services

Functionality

- easy way to help users navigate to the sub areas
- provide human (non-legal) friendly guide sentences with headings to help people choose
- enable user to be able to get where they need in under 15 seconds
- no distractions or alternatives (apart from back)
- enable quick linking to any area of law specialty
- provide access to ask us if you aren't sure option (the only other Call to action on page apart from section links)

Media / Copy Requirements

- headings for each area
- highlighted subsections tht make most sense for users
- guide copy for each area

Amendments

Note that in my mind I have an idea of how this might look.

I am not guiding that here, as my role isn't to design how it looks, and if I get prescriptive I can only get back what I ask for. So I am just trying to design the purpose, the result, and the experience.

If I look at other legal sites as an example, I can see similar pages with just links and links or tables of links, so the user is confronted with a wall of links, not assistance.

I want the page (and all content on it) to be something the user would find useful and helpful.

I added a cheeky sub-goal in it about how long a user will spend on this page, but that is part of the functional design.

If the designer ends up adding a bunch of visual distractions and doesn't pay attention to what we need, then everyone loses out.

Hopefully, the development team and others will ask, "How can we achieve this?" Then you know you have built a useful scoping brief. Now you have people thinking about 'how' and not just slapping it together.

I am going to tackle Wills, one of the Personal Law areas.

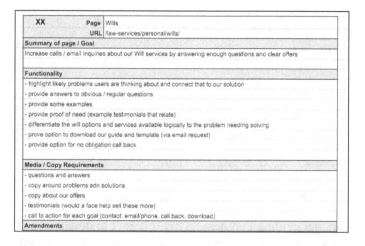

As you progress through all the subpages of your site, it gets harder to be distinctive.

When you come back to these to flesh them out relating to content, you are going to want to list much more detail than this to help everyone understand – whether you do that with a link to a related document of content that thoroughly outlines it or by building out the functionality.

For example, highlight likely problems:

- Don't know where to start on getting a will?
- Has someone in your family died and you are confused about the will options?

By addressing these up front you help people understand what it is that you offer without a bland list like:

The Personal Law Will Services we offer are:

- Creating and updating wills
- Contesting someone's will
- etc.

Rather than hiding FAQs on a topic in a general FAQ section, by blending them in as part of your content and options you are providing useful information in an easily digestible format.

In this instance I am getting specific about content as an example, the scope sheet doesn't need to be a complete piece of content, but you can use examples if they help differentiate this from another page.

You may then determine that the issues and content raised on this topic mean you want to separate the content into more pages – Contesting Wills, Preparing Your First Will, etc. If so, update the sitemap, create more templates, and away you go.

Finishing Steps.

To finish up this chapter, here is how to tidy up what we have created when you are at the end point of this document.

Back to Numbering

Now is the time to lock in the numbering both on your sitemap and this scope document.

In our example:

On each worksheet:

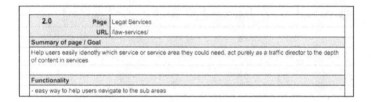

Note that I have now changed the page number to match 2.0.

Tip: In Spreadsheets, 2.0 will get rounded out to 2 by default so rather than worrying about changing the number formatting, and because we aren't calculating it, enter it with a single quotation mark to make it 'text' to the spreadsheet. Thus, 2.0 is entered as '2.0.

In our sitemap:

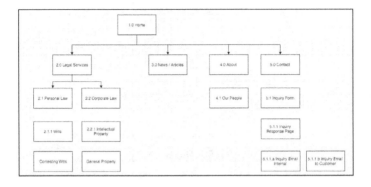

Now that you have done this for every page, it's time to proceed onto the start of the visual process – wireframing.

Skipping to wireframing before now means you are adding shapes and layouts without thought to the function, goal, or content needs, and it won't get the best results.

The result you will produce with this level of scope should be infinitely better.

Resources:

You can download either the word docx version of this template or link through to the google sheet and make your own copy from our Website Planning Guide Resources Page: https://ireck.in/wpgr

10

WIREFRAMING

How To Wireframe Your New Website.

Wireframes are critical to the success of any project because they allow all stakeholders to have critical input early enough to assist in the actual design process. They save time and money, and create a better result.

What Is A Wireframe In Web Design?

A wireframe is a skeletal (bare bones) layout guide for your web pages. It displays the structure of a web page without the use of images or colors or content, so you can see and define the page elements.

By definition:

---

wireframe
/ˈwʌɪəfreɪm/

noun COMPUTING

a skeletal three-dimensional model in which only lines and vertices are represented.

• an image or set of images which displays the functional elements of a website or page, typically used for planning a site's structure and functionality.

Wireframes allow you the ability to define how you see your pages being laid out in advance, before choosing anything else.

Wireframes also help create the foundations you will need to determine your content needs.

Wireframes guide the design process in a way that allows for the important things to be prioritized in your hierarchy of content/elements, so that you get to make critical decisions when they're still easy to change.

Equally important to understand is, **what a wireframe is NOT.**

What a Wireframe isn't

Wireframes **don't usually** involve images, artwork, or color. Once you move into the realm of visual imagery, you aren't working on wireframes you are working on design mock-ups/prototypes that are part of the visual design.

Understanding this difference is very important.

When To Wireframe?

Wireframing should follow the scope phase, so that you are wireframing what you need, not inventing on the fly.

Wireframing is an important part of achieving the best end result. Not because more steps necessarily make a site better, but for you to take control of the process of what your site needs to be.

Many people hand over all control of the design process to the designers.

While that may seem to make sense, in many instances you

are assuming that the designer has the skills to achieve the best result for your business.

Many web designers are front-end visual designers who ultimately draw inspiration from themes or other designers' work. Don't fault them for that, we don't need to reinvent the wheel here, and also many business decision-makers similarly choose their website's end result based on what they like about someone else's site.

If you don't understand 'why' something exists in a design you copy, it can mean it doesn't have any impact for your business if you apply it to your site's design.

I recommend you don't over-control the actual visual design process. The justification for that, apart from two decades of experience of how wrong that can go, is knowing that if you spend the time in research, wireframing, and content you will be much happier with handing over the reins to the design team, because you will know they have everything they need to give you an end product you will love.

How To Wireframe.

A piece of paper is a great starting point, and I will still often do the first sketch there and move to a digital copy later.

There are numerous methods and tools for drafting up wireframes electronically, and you can choose the method that suits you the best.

No need for you to purchase an app or piece of software unless you are going to be producing wireframes regularly.

I usually use Balsamiq, which is a great app and fast for me to utilize. I have also used Word or PowerPoint to do the exact same thing. Unfortunately, I found PowerPoint is too restrictive in the size of screen, so for many people Word or Google Docs will be more than suitable.

Don't get bogged down in the tool you will use, and don't be overly concerned about exactness or whether your wireframe 'looks as good' as a designer's. A wireframe is instructional and isn't an exercise in design.

Tips:

- Create a page template (basic outline) that you can re-use over and over
- Start with a simple outline; reflect later on the hierarchy and priorities
- To begin with, think more in terms of what needs to be included in the page and what doesn't
- Ignore other sites 'looks' and learn more from their 'layout'

Page Layout Basics.

Starting Point

The base page layout. For most sites you will be utilizing something similar to the layout below for the overall page.

Desktop view:

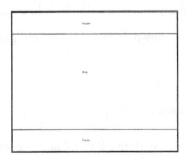

This convention tends to stand true for pages designed for desktops and most of our needs would easily be contained with it.

The Header is what users see first, and typically holds branding assets, primary navigation, and key devices involved in consistent user interaction (e.g. search, shopping cart, contact info, etc).

The Body is where most of the dynamic content will live and where much of the user interaction takes place.

The Footer is the base and end of the page, which might contain less critical information but useful nonetheless. It may hold links to items that reinforce the header or encourage general interaction with less obvious resources.

On mobile/responsive this still works, however the complexity comes later as you start to design for multiple viewpoints and your pages get more involved.

While this is practical for laying out what a page contains, invariably your key wireframes will be built from the top down and be as long as you need them to be.

For the purpose of my wireframing, I use a grid divisible by three that matches the way we invariably design and build things, so they are responsive and friendly in multiple sizes, and allow for sizing that is practical to hold content.

In the examples shown from Balsamiq, my grid is 18 units across.

Wireframing Process.

The full process summary:

1. Initial wireframe, simple lines/shapes, no additional shading or color. Desktop version
2. Review wireframe referring to key materials already

developed (e.g. research, must-haves, scope pages, audience information, and other data

3. Refine layout and work on mobile versions of the same page, including steps 1 and 2 again
4. Refine layout, insert priorities visually (bolding, highlighting, shades)
5. Finalize shading and highlighting, and add examples if necessary to finish the wireframe
6. Rinse and repeat

Note: Due to the way most people make decisions, I have given desktop the priority in how things are laid out. I don't believe this is the correct order specifically (less so in recent years) but it is workable and no one gets excited over a narrow layout mockup for a phone. Sometimes reality needs to be held in check to help you get the task done, which means providing key stakeholders something they can understand.

A Working Example.

Let's put this into practice using the Legal Services example in our scope.

The Contact Page

Create the top of the page, focusing more on the key structural elements rather than the detail, which will come later.

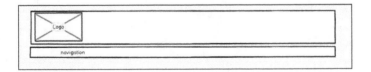

Our header has been split now to show the navigation bar.

While this tends to indicate that a horizontal navigation bar will be used in the actual design, that isn't necessarily the case. Despite what you build in your wireframes, actual detailed design discussions will still take place with your design team (assuming they're fully engaged) about the best method to implement the navigational device you are laying out.

We aren't adding in actual navigational elements (menu items) at this point and there is still much room that may need filling in the header and navigation bar, but this gets us underway.

We are aiming for the big rocks first, little rocks come into the process when we have identified our most important elements and those that are needed.

Keeping in mind our primary goal/purpose for this page:

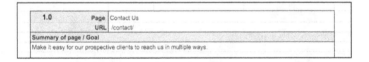

and the multiple ways mentioned that are listed in our functionality list:

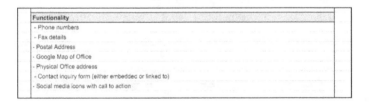

We want to place those item blocks into our page and move them around until we are happy with how these two elements work together.

The evaluation for this page is that there are two primary methods of contact we want to drive: Phone and Email inquiry.

All other forms are of a lower priority to us and less effective, and Fax is something important in legal transactions but not a primary item. It needs to be present but not too dominant.

Our location is important too.

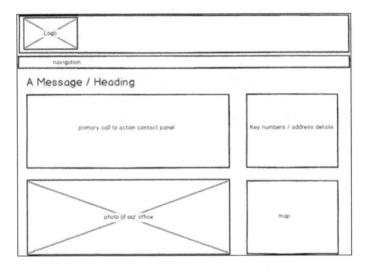

At this point we are simply putting boxes and lines in place. Hopefully the Key numbers box is obvious.

Typically, a design would put the photo at the top and make it the 'feature/highlight' of the page and everything else underneath.

If we stay true to what we have already identified as most important, then the photo is of much lower importance (and only a suggestion at this point). This form of layout helps us see if it's even practical to keep.

Remember this page has a BIG purpose and that's to get inquiries. If the photo doesn't help, then remove it. If it helps with a secondary or third goal then keep it, but use it where it needs to be.

Look at how the mobile version of this page would look:

The top half:

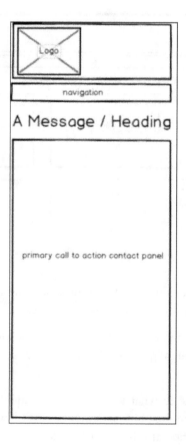

The lower half

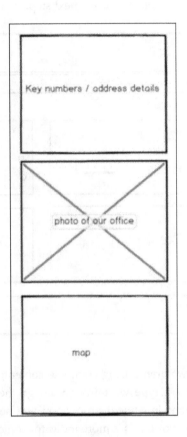

Imagine if we had the office photo at the top. On most typical smartphones and smaller devices all you would see would be that image and the header.

Not a result driven or user-friendly experience at all.

Bring In More Detail.

In our current example here is the next step:

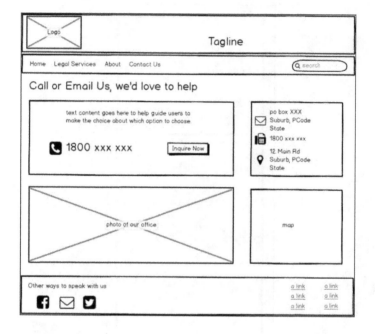

At this stage, we aren't using complete content; we are indicating the content type we think would go there. Knowing full well someone in content production will need to review each and every word, this is more indicator content that helps everyone understand intent.

Using Balsamiq, the icons and options I have chosen are in some instances heavier in color than desired.

When building wireframes of this type, shades of black and their weight tend to emphasize the priority of elements.

Consequently, some of the icons are weighted heavier than I would like e.g. the footer is definitely not as important as the higher elements in this view.

Right click on an icon to view properties. You can change color and other settings in there.

By changing the color weights to lighter shades, I am able to indicate the visual hierarchy without bringing in color. I realize my role isn't to choose colors; I want my professional designers handling that. Using 'Shades of Grey' will help them understand quickly what I value as important.

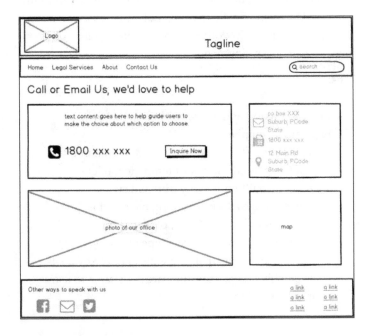

The changes are subtle but very important.

Progressively you are building out each page, element by element, and considering the 'for who, what and why' about each and every element as you go.

Staying with the 'every page has a purpose' philosophy and 'designing' the best way to achieve this goal is the key area of design that needs your input.

You don't have to understand if it's technically possible, easy or hard, you need to understand if it's important or not.

My view is that if most stakeholders who want new results for their websites got to this box-only phase in the scoping process, more projects would end up with better/more successful results.

The following steps are the cream and add more depth to the process. Do them, do them well, but also understand that getting to this point in your process of wireframing for every page is a major development.

Tips:

- Make a desktop and a mobile version for each key page/page template
- Every page needs to be designed – don't fall into the trap of using a bulk standard template model
- Sites can be built with many different styles
- Treat every page as a key landing page that is the key to the success of the next step, or its failure
- If you design a repetitive page type (e.g. blog post) then only wireframe up a single instance of key areas – post, archive page, etc. These are acceptable to use a template model for

11

CONTENT IS KING

C **ontent Is King – Plan Your Website Content.**
Don't leave the most important part of your site to chance. Plan and produce high-quality content.

Your Content Is More Important Than the Design

In many ways, the words you use and how you use them is more important than the visual design you apply to your site.

With so many sites now replicating each other's look, and even elements, your content is most likely going to be the differentiator from your competitors. If you apply this reliable approach to building something purpose driven and useful, then your site will become something that simply works better.

When we refer to content, we are not only talking about the text that fills up the bulk of your pages or posts. All of the words on your site, images, and multimedia also make up your site content.

Content's Role in Your Business

Understanding where content fits into your whole business

marketing system helps to understand its role in better serving your clients' needs.

Instead of seeing content as just words and images, think of the role it plays and evaluate its importance based on how critical that role is.

Different types of content can fill roles such as:

- Education – answering questions about the kind of product or service you offer
- Customer Support – guiding your existing clients on how to get support through your business
- Search Engine – in its simplest form, getting found on Search Engines for specific topics can't happen if you don't have the relevant content
- Trust – providing quality content helps to build confidence in your brand and your service
- Sales – handling sales objections up front as well as logical funnel processes helps guide prospects to make a purchase from your business
- After Sales – quality mail (paper and email) adds to your business marketing process and helps to ensure a smooth customer experience

There are a myriad of ways content fulfils critical roles in your company that directly affect how successful your site will be.

You cannot afford to take the role of content lightly. It should have as much attention throughout the entire build process as the design.

Content Must Have a Purpose.

Throughout this process, we have been highlighting how important it is to focus on the goal/purpose for every part of your website.

When you consider what content will be required, and also when that content is produced, you must always adhere to this way of thinking, otherwise you will undermine all the other work you have put into the project.

As Sally Bagshaw, Content Strategist from **Web Content Strategy,** outlines:

"The most important thing you can do is have a very clear vision of how content will help you meet your business goals by fulfilling your customers' needs. Is your content there to inspire them? Educate them? Or assist them to complete a task? It's better to launch a site with a small amount of thoughtfully planned quality content that you can evolve over time, than a bunch of pages that don't serve a particular purpose."

The goal for any piece of content doesn't necessarily have to be obvious, such as a Call to Action, but it should be deliberate.

You should have a reason for creating a case study. Why have you chosen this subject to write about and why is it being used? What message is it delivering, what are you trying to achieve, why did you choose these images?

SEO Research for Content.

A critical part of developing your content needs is best served with traditional Search Engine Optimization (SEO) research.

This research is a key part of multiple areas of this guide including Research, Scoping, and Content. You need to make sure you use SEO research if you want to fully develop a result-driven brief.

Ed Pelgen from Online Kickstart explains it like this:

"SEO is simply about making sure your website pages and blog posts get found when your prospects are searching online for a product or a solution to their problem.
To understand the fundamentals of SEO in site development you can find some fantastic resources including MOZ's Beginners Guide to SEO as well as plenty of informative articles and guides on conducting Keyword Research."

Using Keyword Research techniques will assist you in creating unique pages of content on your site to match user needs, and improve your content types and categories based around how people search for your products or services.

Using this knowledge will also assist in creating more user-friendly and logical site structures and URLs.

There are a number of paid and free Keyword Research tools; some of the common ones are Google Adwords, Keyword Planner, and Ubersuggest.

Planning Your Content.

When you wrote your first draft scope of the site, you will already have identified a lot of content elements needed to write or create, and the reason for them.

Now you need to collate all the specifications for particular content types into useful lists that you can give to the people who will produce the content.

You should separate content into the type e.g. written, images, or video, and make sure you outline the exact requirements.

If you are going to be engaging an external copywriter, it will be important for both them and your budget that you organize these requirements. Allowing them to quantify how much is required, and have a real insight into its purpose will ensure an accurate quote, budget, and timeline for production.

Internally you can start to gauge how much time it will take to pull the content together.

It is extremely common for a design agency to undertake the project with an expectation that the content will hold up the delivery of the project, and it's rare that even draft content is ready for the initial briefing phase.

If you can compile the requirements for content and commence production you are going to be a long way ahead in the process of completing the end product.

Make sure you include all the content you will need including email responders, on-screen thank you messages, and other automated content items. List out Social Media image styles that you might need for blog posts, and icons for the different social accounts you have.

All of these elements make up the overall Content Master List for your site.

Content Master List.

You are going to need a Content Requirements Master List. This list is in its simplest form a table of content required.

You can make this as complicated or as simple as suits your needs, projects, and how many people are on the team. I recommend you at least outline the individual requirements per page (e.g. Images, Body Copy, Call to Action) over simply listing the page as needing content.

When you start collating and producing the content, it is very easy to lose track of what is in draft state, final state, and even things missed.

This is a sample table view to create a list:

- **Item** – Just a number so you can reference things if needed
- **Type** – I use a drop down here of pre-defined items so you can pick from them. These are easy to add in Google Sheets by right clicking and choosing Data Validation. You can then copy it down the list and select individually (see below)
- **Page** – The page name from your sitemap
- **Reference** – When you number the sitemap, you can cross-reference that number in here
- **Description** – A simple summary of requirements. Detail will exist elsewhere in the scope documents
- **Status** – R= Requested, D = Draft (received), F = Final (received)

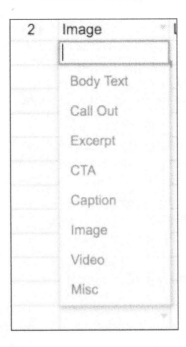

This is a guide only and is intended to show a method that will help you stay on top of all of the content items needed to complete your project.

You will build this Master List by working your way through the scope document, sitemap and wireframes. In each instance, you will cross-reference that each part of that document group has relevant items. Where you see new requirements that you add to this Master List, you need to add it to the corresponding scope page or another document so that they are all accurate and up to date.

This is the final step in making sure each part of the process iscomplete. Items that you may have skipped over quickly in the scope document, because you needed more answers or clarity, should be filled out in more detail now.

There are some great online content collaboration tools available and we often use Gather Content, which allows us to create templates to re-use for certain content types. You can set statuses and lock content when finalized, which you can then provide to the design team as finished and approved documents.

Whichever method you use, you need a managed repository for version control, a naming convention for documents and images, etc. so that you can find them, and good discipline in creating folders and placing items in there ready for use on the project. You may wish to record on the Master List the name of whoever provided the content to help manage changes, etc.

Give Content Budget and Time.

If you want a high-performing website, you need to ensure you allocate adequate time to the preparation and production of all content.

This includes a suitable budget. As Sally's quote highlights, you are better to have high-quality content in smaller amounts than lots of thin and poorly prepared content. If you have a tight budget, use it wisely and produce only essential content that will impact your results favorably.

If you can't afford a copywriter and custom photography in the initial stages, then choose good quality and non-generic stock photography or illustrations carefully, and get your copy right. Then come back later and further enhance with better photography or illustrations.

Be realistic; it's important to understand the significant impact that the right words, image, or device in the right place can have on how your website is used, and consequently the results it generates.

12

THE DOCUMENT

Completing Your Website Brief

I t's time to bring it all together into a brief for your project.

Compiling the Documents

Now is the time to do a final check and create a document that will provide anyone quoting or working on your project a complete picture of what you want and why you want it.

In your final brief, you are going to bring together a series of pages and documents that step through the background behind the project, the research completed for the project, your goals and targets for the project, and all of the detail you have put into the scope pieces.

This chapter completes the core of this guide and will give you more than enough information and knowledge to proceed through the development stages.

If you have reached this stage, you should congratulate yourself. You have invested time that many others don't. You won't be someone that wonders how their project got away from them. You will be able to see a successful project through to completion.

Your Finished Brief

Keep in mind that this document will have many people who need to use it.

It is the master plan for your site, the brief for your design and development team, a guide for your content producers, an approval document for key stakeholders, and much more.

It needs to have a clear structure that anyone can follow and thereby get a comprehensive understanding of the project.

When you bring it all together your Brief/Scope should include the following items:

- Goals
- Audience Outline
- Must-have Requirements
- Research Summary
- Sitemap
- Scope document
- Wireframes
- Content Outline

1. The Introduction

This written introduction should explain to anyone reviewing the project, answers to the following questions:

- Why is this project happening?
- What expectations are there for this project?
- Are there any references to existing materials? (e.g. existing websites)

- Who are the key contacts and stakeholders from your business related to this project?

One page is probably enough to outline these important points. While the objective of this scoping process is to provide more detail about your project, we want the readers to be spending time on the main detail and not going through repetitive content in each area.

2. Goals

This page or two of content should come directly from what you prepared in the Goal Setting chapter. As you went through the scoping process, you would have refined the wording and specificity of the goals.

Review them and include them here. It is worthwhile to include a statement about goals and their importance for all concerned, i.e., "That all decisions made are meant to create a purpose that achieves these goals; anything else is a distraction."

Set the guidelines up front, then if your suppliers or team get distracted by shiny gadgets or options you can consistently bring them back to the question:

"How does this help us achieve our goals?"

3. Audience Outline

How much content you have in this section will depend on how in depth you have gone in building audience personas, and how much research you have done.

It would be ideal that you devote several pages here to providing top-level summaries of your audience and provide full details as part of supplementary documentation when required.

In initial reviews by prospective agencies or design teams, they may be happy with the summary level detail, and it will help both parties get through the first round of selections. They may or may not need to see the full detail until they have been commissioned.

If you only have one or two audience profiles and a very clear history of serving them, then you should outline them clearly here, and make sure everyone understands who this site is for.

4. Must-Have Requirements

In Chapter 5, you listed out any specific requirements you need this website project to have for your business.

These need to be outlined here, and reference where in other scope documentation that the full detail exists. This page or two should highlight everything that needs to be included and enough information to make it meaningful.

For example, "Our existing user forum http://community.businessdomain.com will be retained and key topics will be extracted and displayed on the page in our new sitemap '12.1 Community Topics'. Full API and Feed information are provided in the scope documentation. The existing version of this can be seen at:

http://www.domain.com/oldpage"

This summary of an item will alert everyone to enough specifics without getting bogged down in technical elements. These should be handled further in the document.

Emphasize everything you know must be included.

5. Research Summary

When presenting what you have learned from conducting research, you won't need to display and outline everything you did and went through unless you are unsure as to the conclusions your research provides.

Ultimately the research should create some clear information that guides each of the scoping phases, including determining the architecture of the site, content needs, functional requirements, and design needs.

In this section, you want to detail the key lessons and messages that shone through in your research, which have guided the rest of this brief. The readers of the brief should be able to get a strong sense of why decisions they will read about later have been made, what problems they need to solve in reaching the goals, and what they need to reference when you get to approval and testing stages.

6. Sitemap

Depending on the size of your site, you may have a one-page sitemap or multiple pages. If you used a tool like draw.io or Visio, then export them as image files or PDF pages, and include these into your website brief document.

Ensure each page of the sitemap is labeled and include text references to subpages where relevant, so readers can easily make the connections between the different maps. Check your numbering is correct and every item in the scope is included.

7. Page Scope Document

Whether you include this in your brief document or not will depend on size and the software you used to create it.

If you used Google Sheets, you can make a copy which is Read-Only and share that link in this overall document. That way you won't have a bloated document to send.

If you made it in Word or Excel or similar tools, then PDF it and include it in the final documents. You need to make sure each tab/page scoped is included, and any notations are shown on each page.

8. Wireframes

You will need to export all your wireframes as images or PDF documents. If you have it all in Balsamiq, you can export the entire project in one go, which saves a lot of time.

If you create a PDF, then you can merge this PDF file into your master PDF if you intend to have it as one document.

Alternatively, the wireframes can be stored as a separate file and referenced in the main brief document. If you have a large number of wireframes, the export will be a large file so storing it separately will be helpful for those that need to access it.

9. Content Outline

The content outline should add some detail to the scope document by explaining more about the type of content production, who is producing it or if you need someone to do this, references to any Content Style Guides you may have, and expected production timeframes for the content.

You should also include the Content Master Plan.

This will allow everyone to see the size and shape of all the content requirements and to understand the importance of content in your project.

It won't be considered an afterthought.

The Brief.

If your site is going to be ten pages or more, this brief will now include quite a lot of documentation.

Creating an online folder that can be shared with any prospective developers will make good sense, e.g. Dropbox, drive, or similar. In the folder, you can place each of the main files and the overall guide that makes up the brief.

This way the summary brief outlined on this page will be the initial document, and will reference the other large documents.

When you have brought this all together, you will have done what many people never invest enough time into. You will have built a full blueprint and guide for your web project.

You now have the keys to your success. You won't be leaving the critical decisions up to your developers; you will have provided the design and content teams with a plethora of useful information that allows them to do their job more easily.

Not only will you know what your end project will ultimately be like when completed, but it will also be completely purpose driven, and easy to quote and put a project plan to, because there won't be any missing pieces or ambiguity.

If you find an agency or developer that can't give you a fixed price and a timeline to build this project, I would suggest you probably have someone you don't really want to work with.

What's Next?

This completes the scoping and briefing side of this guide. This is the main content we wanted to produce to help you build a better website and be more successful with your online projects.

We also have a **Facebook group** exclusively for people who have bought either a printed or ebook version of this book. We offer instructions, help and additional information as well as an opportunity to get your questions answered there.

Join the group:

https://www.facebook.com/groups/websiteplan/

We would love to hear from you and learn how this guide has helped you scope and deliver better web projects. You can follow us on Twitter @ireckon or email us info@ireckon.com.

A NOTE FROM DARRYL

Thanks for taking the time out of your busy life to read this book.

I hope you were able to see a way on how you can plan web projects better.

It's tough on both sides of the table (agency/developer and client) because everyone needs to get there quick. Or so we are told.

What I'd like to challenge you to do is to understand how taking shortcuts upfront means higher long-term costs, in money, frustration and lost business.

You don't have to write a 100,000-word masterpiece, but the process of putting into a brief your ideas will always be better than an ad-lib approach.

There's a lot more to the best websites than just what is in this book. I didn't want to give you the simple basics that are out there in abundance, nor dig so deep on elements of marketing that you didn't take action. I think this is a good compromise on how to plan your sites better.

I'd love to get your feedback, either in the form of reviews wherever you bought this book or by connecting with me online.

You can reach me best on twitter (@ireckon) or our Facebook group (https://www.facebook.com/groups/websiteplan/) which you get free access to, via email through www.websiteplanningguide.com; sign up for the reader's insights there, where I will be providing insights on the chapters and examples of what we do in practice in our workshops.

I'm developing several additional information resources, including a look from both agencies and clients on working together through the development process.

You'll find out about that and some exciting tools we are developing by joining that list.

I'd love to hear how you have used the guide in your next projects.

If you have any issues accessing the free templates, please reach out, I'm here to help you build better websites.

Darryl King

ABOUT THE AUTHOR

Darryl King is the founder of Ireckon, an Australian based Web Design and Development Agency based in Brisbane.

He has been actively involved in the scoping, planning and project management of thousands of web projects.

The Complete Guide to Planning a Website was born from the frustrations and problems the lack of proper brief documents caused for both his development teams as well as for clients.

After searching and trying many different functional specification documents, advertising briefs and other simplistic website planning tools that barely skimmed the surface of what clients need to provide, he developed and tested The Complete Guide to Website Planning.

Darryl uses the advanced version of this process in his consulting with clients to develop their website scoping documents and plans.

He also conducts workshops, site audits and does speaking events to encourage a more thorough approach to website planning.

Connect with Darryl online:

www.websiteplanningguide.com

(twitter) @ireckon

Darryl's Fiction site: www.kingdarryl.com

ACKNOWLEDGMENTS

Thanks to all the clients over more than twenty years that have helped in creating this system and provided the knowledge and learnings that make up the content of this book.

Special mention should go to the many team members over the years who pushed me to find a better way to help them do a better job.

For the ongoing encouragement to push this to completion and make it happen, a shoutout to Ed Pelgen of Online Kickstart.

And importantly thanks to my wife Gill who has always been in my corner encouraging me.

The Complete Website Planning Guide Workbook

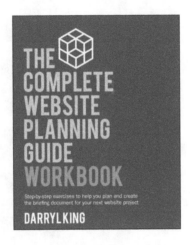

The companion Workbook which expands on this book.

- Each section has exercises to guide you through the planning process and examples
- Enhanced detail on every step of the process
- Additional downloads to complement each of the exercises

Available in Print format from all good bookstores.